To Janet
thank you for
being an Amazing
mentor and friend.
I love you and appreciate
you. Thanks for your
friendship.

Love,
Keiona

"Because a little help always goes a long way and is always remembered"

~Keiona~

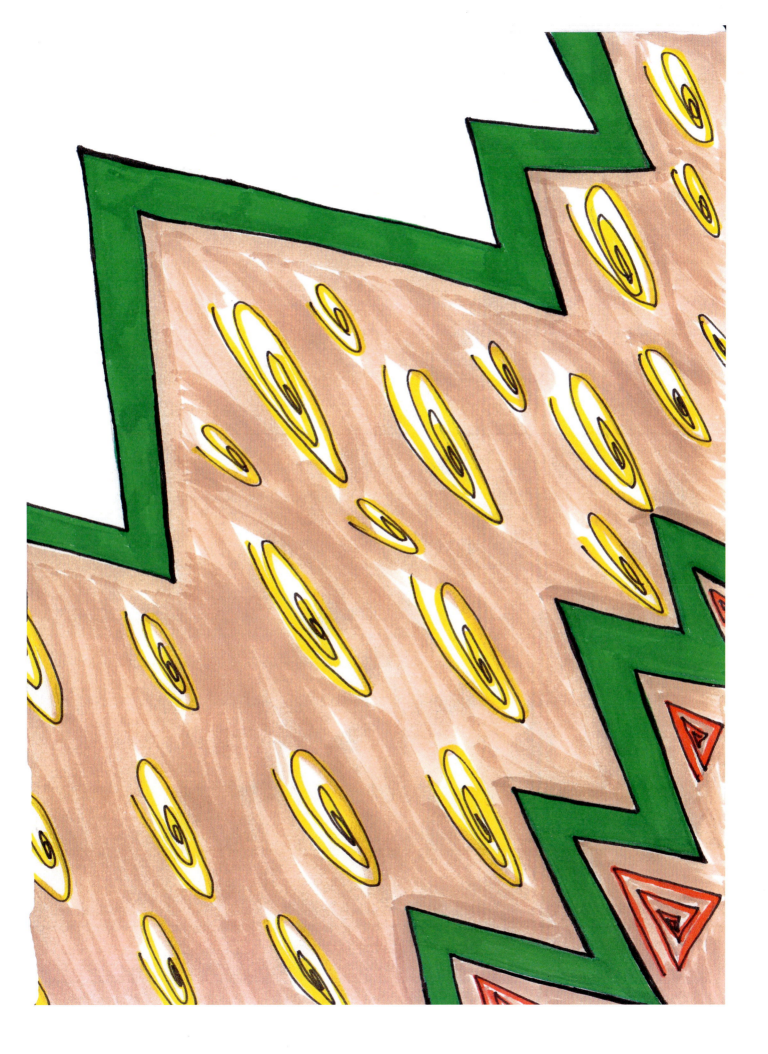

A special thank you to the amazing
editors, family and friends who helped edit this
enchanting book.

To my friend Janet Donaldson, an artist, former newspaper reporter, editor and publisher of women's history curriculum, thank you for taking me under your wings to support all my dreams.

To my friend Dawn Duncan Harrell, graduate of Houghton College. Former editor at Hendrickson Publishing, she is currently the publisher and author of DC Harrell Books.Many thank you.

To my friend Ms. Pat thank you as well, for helping to critique and give ideas to grow the collection of books to come.

Written and Illustrated by Keiona L. Cook
Self-published and printed through www.createspace.com in the United States of America

This book is dedicated to my son Ken and our
continued relationship of growth as a mother and son.

This book is also dedicated to all the
children of Lovely's Sewing & Arts Collective
and children of the world as a eye-opener into the
daily tasks of their parents.

Always show the best verison of yourself to
yourself and to the world, because someone is always
secretly looking up to you, both the young and old.

~Keiona Cook~

Lovely
Helps
Mommy
Fold the
Laundry

"Mommy do you need help with anything today? You know how good of a helper I can be. So do you need help with anything?" says, Lovely.

"Lovely, What are you up to? I know you're up to something," says Mommy.

"I'm not up to anything, Mommy. I just want to help you out around the house."

"Movies and the ice cream parlor would be great on such a sunny afternoon," Lovely whispers under her breath.

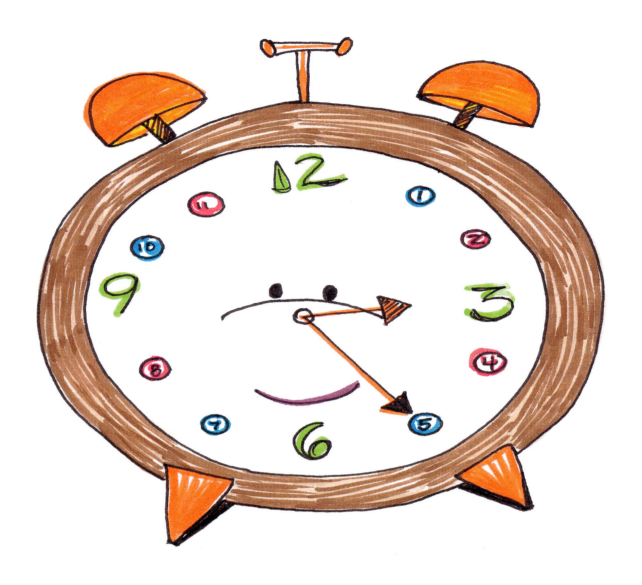

"Well, Lovely you can help me fold the laundry after I take my 25 minute power nap," says Mommy.
"Hooray," says Lovely.

"Now kids, if the current time is 3:25 pm and Mommy is taking a 25 minute nap, what time will it be in 25 minutes?" _____
"If you guessed 3:50 pm, you're right," said Lovely.

"Let's start by checking the clean clothes basket. The less Mommy has to do, the more time she will have to spend with me. I can just taste the ice cream," says Lovely daydreaming.

"Okay, so there are six face towels, two hand towels, and one bath towel in the basket. Let's get started with Mommy's magic folding way," said Lovely.

Mommy's Magical Folding

How to Fold the Face Towel

Step 1: Lay the towel down on a flat surface and smooth out the edges.

Step 2: Fold the towel in half and smooth the edges.

Step 3: Fold the towel in half again, the short way. If you have the perfect square, you folded the towel just right.

How to Fold the Hand Towel

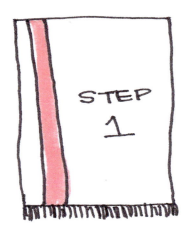

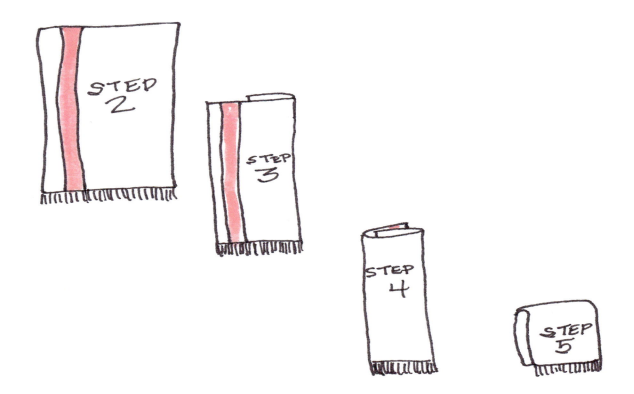

Step 1: Lay the towel down on a flat surface with the wrong side facing up.

Step 2: Smooth out the edges.

Step 3: Fold the towel over 1/3 of the way.

Step 4: Fold over the other side.

Step 5: Fold the towel over from the top to the bottom.

How to Fold the Bath Towel

Step 1: Lay the towel down on a flat surface. Next smooth out the edges.

Step 2: Fold the towel in half.

Step 3: Fold the towel in half again.

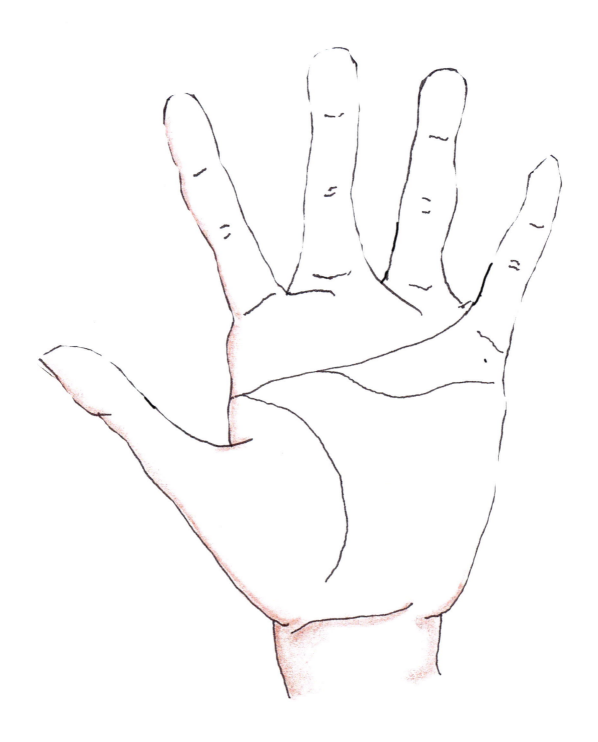

"Amazing job folding the towels with me kids. Give yourself a pat on the back, kids and give me a high five," says Lovely.

"Now let's check the dryer," said Lovely.

"Ohhhh, it's stuck, this blanket just won't come out," yells Lovely in frustration.

"Lovely what are you doing?" says Mommy

"Surprise, Mommy! I folded all the clean clothes. Now can you help me with this blanket; it's stuck?" says Lovely.

"Yes baby, good job being a great helper," says Mommy.

Step 1: Grab the corners of the blanket with your index fingers and thumbs.

Step 2: Fold the blanket in half by putting the corners of the blanket together.

Step 3: Grab the blanket that is hanging down and repeat the second step again.

Step 4: Carefully bring the corners of your blanket up to your partner, in my case Mommy. Then grab the corners that are hanging down.

Step 5: Carefully bring the corners up to Mommy one last time.

Also give Mommy or your partner a hug for a job well done.

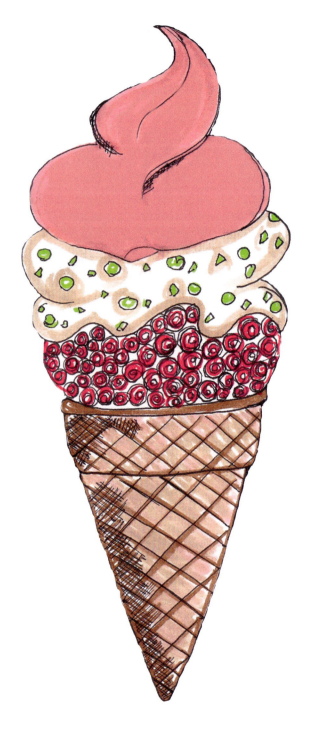

"Mommy, we did it! Now can we go get
ice cream and go see a movie, Please," says Lovely.

"Lovely, I knew you were up to something. Now I appreciate you helping around the house, but don't think this means you're going to get something in return, everytime you help around the house. Ice cream in the kitchen and a movie in the living room. Great job helping with the laundry today," says Mommy.

"I love Mommy time. I will have to help Mommy around the house more. Sometimes she is sooo tired after a long day at work, and anything I can do to help her, will also make me very happy," said Lovely.

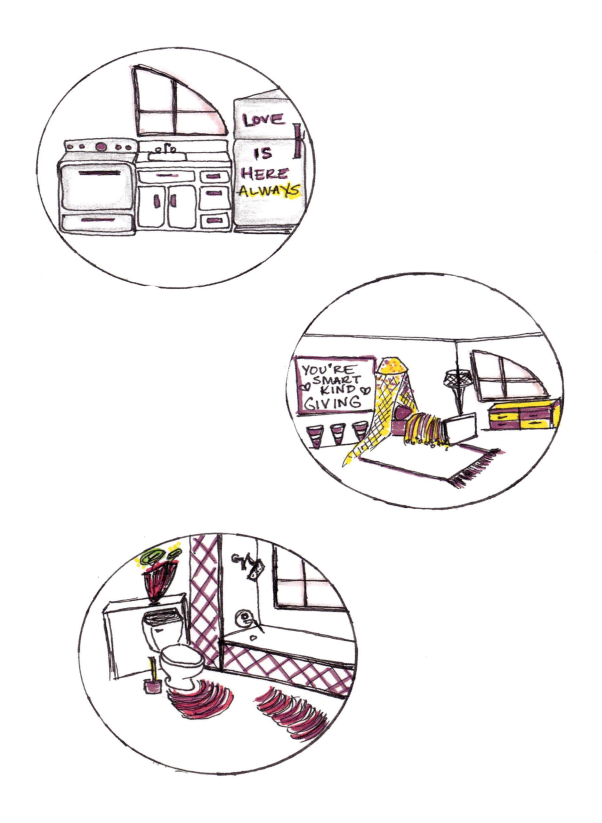

"I can show Mommy I appreciate her by keeping my room clean and by helping keep other rooms in the house clean too. The less Mommy has to do, the more time we can spend together. Hooray! She can teach me everything she knows! And we will sneak in fun Mommy time too, says Lovely.

Movie Loading
>>>>>>

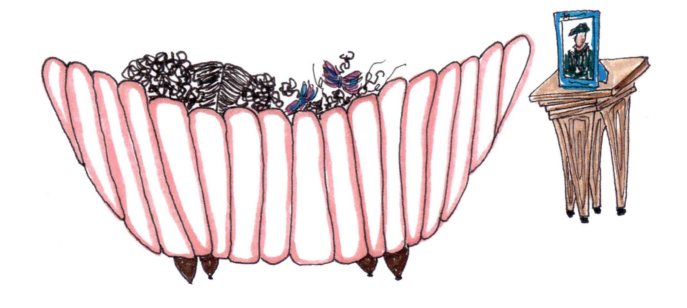

"Mommmy, I wish daddy were here?" says Lovely.
"Don't worry, he will be home in two weeks. Until then hold onto his smile and courage as he fights for our country," says Mommy

"Awwwww, I love mommy time," says Lovely.

"See you soon Daddy," says Lovely.
Commander James Johnson of the Army Air Force tactical unit.

Parents
&
Kids
Meet the Author

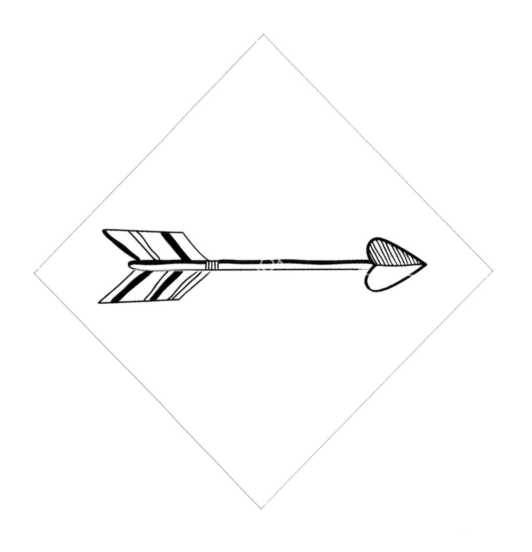

Keiona Cook is a native of Chicago, IL and has made North Minneapolis, MN her current Minniapple in the sky. Keiona is a Performing Arts Teacher in Minneapolis. She teaches sewing, yoga, dance, poetry and public speaking through her nonprofit organization Lovely's Sewing & Arts Collective (LSAC) established in June of 2010. www.lovelyssewing.org

As a child Keiona was always mommies little helper fascinated with the idea of learning something new everyday. By being a good helper she learned to draw very well, clean, cook and also give without always expecting something in return.

Keiona is a giver, that continues to give out of the kindness of her heart. She wrote this book to encourage kids to be helpers and givers without being a selfish seeker.

"Always do your best, because you are important and you are loved dearly."

~Keiona~

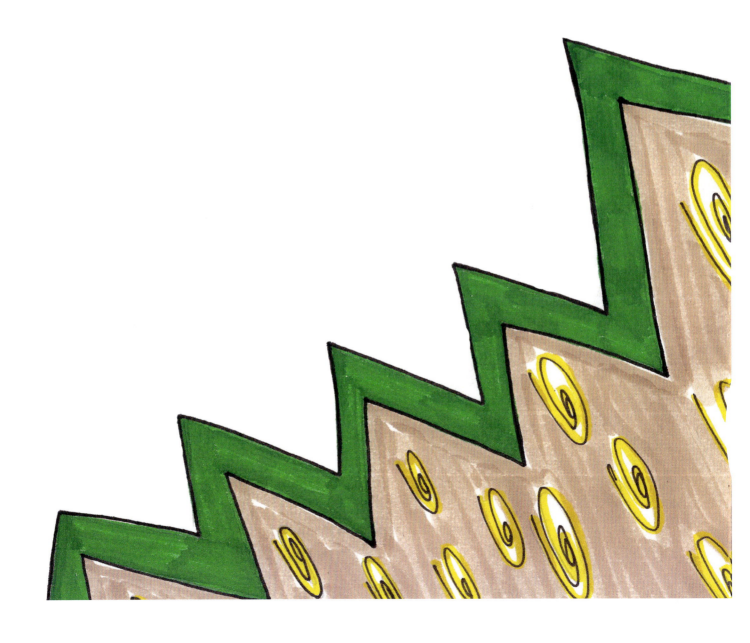

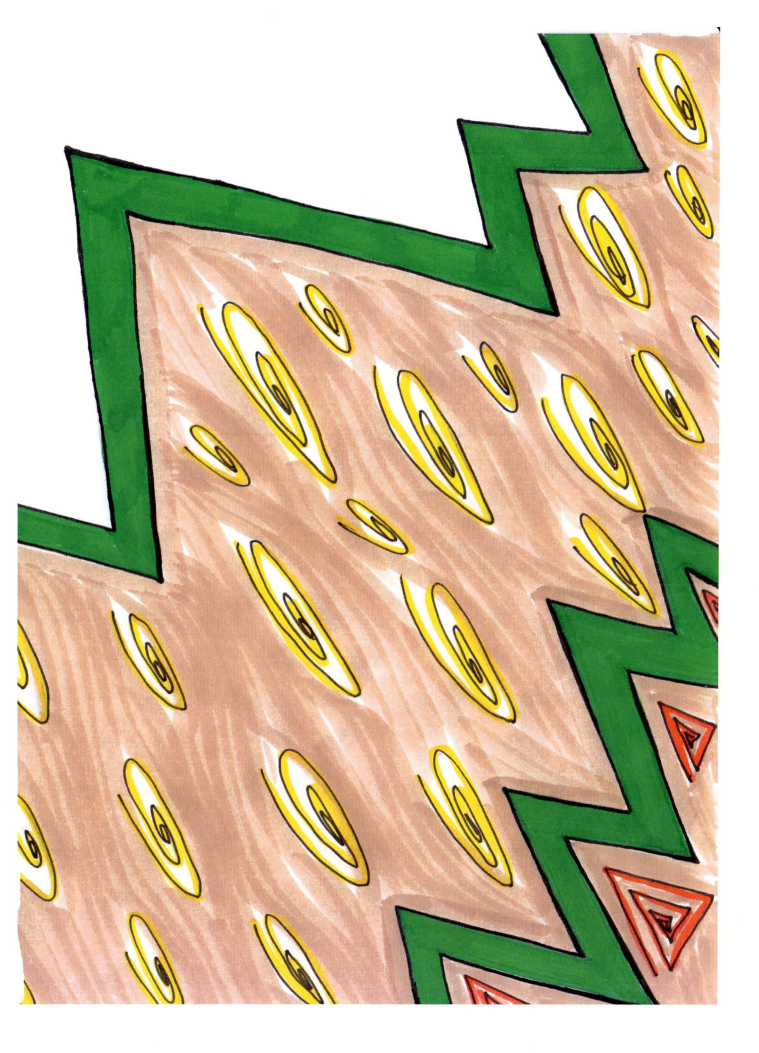

✳✳

Kids how can you be a Great Helper around the house?

_____

_____

_____

_____

_____

_____

_____

Parents how can you spend more time with your kids?

_____

_____

_____

_____

_____

89314922R00020

Made in the USA
Lexington, KY
26 May 2018